Olek Netzer

Person-Centered Political Party

New Ways of Democracy

Volume 8

LIT

Olek Netzer

Person-Centered Political Party

A Blueprint for Organization Free of Power Corruption

LIT

Front cover:
The Goddess of Democracy. Replica at the University of British Columbia of the statue made by Chinese students in Beijing in June 1989 and destroyed by the army on the day of Tiananmen Square massacre.

This book is printed on acid-free paper.

Bibliographic information published by the Deutsche Nationalbibliothek
The Deutsche Nationalbibliothek lists this publication in the Deutsche Nationalbibliografie; detailed bibliographic data are available in the Internet at http://dnb.dnb.de.

ISBN 978-3-643-91296-1 (br.)
ISBN 978-3-643-96296-6 (PDF)

A catalogue record for this book is available from the British Library.

Flössergasse 10
CH-8001 Zürich
Tel. +41 (0) 76-632 84 35
E-Mail: zuerich@lit-verlag.ch http://www.lit-verlag.ch
Distribution:
In the UK: Global Book Marketing, e-mail: mo@centralbooks.com
In North America: Independent Publishers Group, e-mail: orders@ipgbook.com
In Germany: LIT Verlag Fresnostr. 2, D-48159 Münster
Tel. +49 (0) 2 51-620 32 22, Fax +49 (0) 2 51-922 60 99, e-mail: vertrieb@lit-verlag.de
e-books are available at www.litwebshop.de

To Tirza

TABLE OF CONTENTS

THE CONTRACT

In the muddy waters of politics, the purpose of this work will be crystal-clear from the beginning: The author assumes the role of an organizational consultant who is a practitioner of Applied Behavioral Science, specifically Organizational Development (OD). He offers his professional expertise on organizational behavior and interpersonal dynamics to readers who wish to become politically empowered, but not power-corrupted, as political Parties.

In the country I live in, I hold strong political convictions and am politically active but as an organizational consultant my political sympathies will not play a role. I do not have any conflict of values with the clients this Blueprint intends to serve wherever they live, because their values and goals are also mine. Political activists who have in mind winning support by using divisive means of propaganda and by power struggle will not find this Blueprint to their taste. However if you, the reader, become convinced that this radical organizational proposal might indeed serve your personal and political tastes values and objectives, you can apply it in your life for your own political goals. The goals of your involvement in politics are yours. My role must be limited to designing the organization's structure and recommending processes most effective for practicing your values and reaching your goals while avoiding power corruption.

The first step, in establishing the consultant-client relationship, is agreeing on a working contract. I shall therefore spell out what are the demands and needs of the other side of this contract, in reality you the reader. The organizational Blueprint intends to answer those wishes and demands. I assume you are well aware of the fact that, to date, all attempts by well-meaning people to organize politically have degenerated into power-corrupted politics and thus have resulted in regimes equally or more tyrannical than the ones they had replaced. In the West, the New Left movements faded out without changing the political power system.

This Blueprint has been designed for clients who understand their need for political organization as rooted in their humanistic values. They demand that their organization will answer their needs and support the actualization of their values, which are the following:

MORALITY, DECENCY

We want our organizational procedures to facilitate and reward decency in interpersonal relations while thwarting machinations, manipulation of others, psychologically exploitative rhetoric, and all sorts of Machiavellian political tactics. We regard these as the most pervasive aspects of Power-Corruption that could corrupt us regardless of our just goals and good intentions.

EQUALITY, DEMOCRACY

We want our organization to be truly democratic, and that means **fundamentally egalitarian**. We want it to be an association of free and equal people who collaborate to achieve their political goals. We insist that the decision-making processes in our movement will prevent as much as possible unequal distribution of organizational power. Ideally, each of us should be equally empowered to make decisions for the entire organization. – We do not wish anyone to dominate other members or feel powerless and insignificant in relation to party chairpersons, leaders, directors, ideologues, or functionaries.

EFFECTIVENESS, EFFICIENCY

We want our political movement to be effective and productive in **making a difference** in our lives, society, environment, country or as far and wide as we choose. We are not interested in wasting our time and energy on a political experience that amounts to no more than a sort of social club or debating society.

AFFINITY, SOLIDARITY, HIGH QUALITY OF ORGANIZATIONAL LIFE

We demand high quality in our political life. We want our **individual political experience to be humanly positive**. We want our organization not just to empower us politically, but also to give each individual member the right and opportunity to be heard, respected and valued. Our organized political experience should keep us personally fulfilled, energized rather than exhausted, motivated to continue our involvement and able **to become a positive model for many others**. We require that our organizational procedures be structured to minimize the chance that individual members could be devalued, manipulated or used by others.

If you, the reader, have those values and needs for your organized political experience, this book is for you. This Blueprint is designed to support each of them. Our hypothetical consultant-client contract is with a client who is seriously committed to democratic, humanistic, person-centered values. The author, in his capacity as professional consultant, provides the best solutions for the client's needs that he could find in validated theories and research on the organizational experience. At long last this Blueprint could finally break the "Power Corrupts" spell.

Person-Centered Political Organization: An Overview

Psychology can be very subversive when it enters the arena of power-politics – Carl Rogers

Organic Web Structure

What organizational arrangements would work efficiently and effectively and promote person-centered democratic-egalitarian values while preventing Power Corruption from invading the organizational body? In answering this question, we first shall briefly overview the whole Blueprint. You will find it no less than a revolutionary departure from the known structures of any existing political Party or movement; in fact, it turns them upside down. Then we shall clarify how each part of this proposed structure promotes equality and empowerment of individuals, works for organizational efficiency and effectiveness, and prevents all aspects of Power Corruption.

The whole organization is designed like a web rather than a pyramid of ascending authority. The organizational chart presents a voluntary partnership of small groups. The full organizational body will be made up of small cells, like any living organism. Each small group will contain a number of members which is limited to allow members to get to know one another, form personal relationships, and meet in an ordinary private home, where each member can talk and listen to all others person-to-person rather than address an audience. In a tribute to some well-intentioned people in the 1960s, this organizational Blueprint refers to small groups that should form its solid building blocks as Affinity Groups.

DECISION MAKING

The main task of the small Affinity Groups would be to make decisions. The Web-Movement will make its decisions *directly*, with all member groups participating routinely. The person-centered political organization will be a network of Affinity Groups, *each group with equal access to the highest level of organizational power*. The Affinity Groups will be interconnected by a delicate fabric of their free-will decisions to belong to the movement, rather than by any chains of bureaucratic dependence.

In the person-centered political Web-Movement, the regular democratic process of decision-making will involve all members in Affinity Groups, not just representatives. In existing political organizations, "Party Line" and all strategic and other important decisions are made by leaders or by The Leader. In our Web, decisions will be made routinely by all members in their Affinity Groups. The Affinity Groups will meet once in one or two weeks; no less than once a month because, like a living organism, groups need a minimal rate of heartbeat and breathing, otherwise they cannot really be alive. All groups will communicate their decisions to a communication center, and decisions approved by a majority of Affinity Groups will become the Party's decisions.

The Web-Movement's executives will not make decisions for the organization. Their role will be to implement decisions made regularly by all members. That stands in contrast to the common political Party routine, in which elected leaders make decisions, and members are given only formal access to the decision-making process, once every few years, by electing their representatives to the Party's convention.

AGENDA SETTING

Affinity Groups will set the organization's agenda. This means that every member of the Web Movement will have *direct* access to power – and that means a *real chance* at all times – to decide what should be the priority issues which the Movement will focus its energy on. What all Affinity Groups are going to decide on in any given round of organizational decision-making will be their choice. The executives could put issues on the agenda too, but with no preferential treatment of their agenda. The whole inter-group agenda setting process can be easily done by electronic communication.

To set the agenda, you can choose a procedure that is best suited to the organization's size. One possible way could be the following: A group that wants to put an item on the organization's agenda sends its motion to a communication center. Staff members in the communication center make a list of all items suggested for the organization's decision-making and send it back to Affinity Groups. Members in all groups then rank-order the items for urgency. The highest ranked items are put on the agenda first in the next round of decision-making.

Another possible arrangement: the task of agenda-setting rotates among the Affinity Groups.

MEMBERSHIP

Membership in an Affinity Group will be the only formal connection of a member to the Web-Movement organization. The group will grant membership status to applying individuals after members had gotten to know them as persons and could form an opinion based on their participation in the group's life. Membership will not be sold for money, as is the accepted way of getting a Party membership card in conventional political organizations. People who want to belong will have to share something of themselves with the group, communicate with others, and accept the group's decisions and regulations in order to become equal members of the small community. Members of the Affinity Group – they alone and no one else – will have the power of decision regarding acceptance, membership, and termination of membership of individuals.

Neither any institution nor any leader outside the Affinity Group will have the right to interfere with accepting and rejecting membership of persons in it. Thus there will be no personal dependency on any Party apparatus ever! In fact, there will be no Party membership in the same sense as today. Individual membership will have meaning only within the small Affinity Group, where members know each other as persons and not just as "Party members" (usually no more than a name on a list with an address and a telephone number). The Person-Centered Web-Movement will be an organization of such human-sized groups, not of people isolated and alienated from one another.

Membership of an Affinity Group in the Web-Movement will be based on the group's participation and compliance with the Web's conditions. A committee of members from other groups, preferably in geographic proximity, will be authorized to decide on matters of granting, renewing or denying membership of an Affinity Group in the Person-Centered political organization. Central executive organs of the Web-Movement will have no authority in matters of belonging to it.

LEADERSHIP: GOOD RIDDANCE!

The Person-Centered condition of equality in sharing organizational power – is incompatible with institutionalized leadership. Life in an organizational environment of personal independence and equality cannot, by definition, be realized in a climate of leaders and followers, party bosses and rank-and-file. Either we are equal or we divide into "Indians and Chiefs". Organizational power-pyramids, which rank-order rather than equalize power, reflect the authoritarian patriarchal experience and, by that, rule out any possibility of realizing the historical aspiration of people for "Fraternity" in their political-social experience.

Institutionalized leadership authorizes some people to use power and denies that authority to others. Hierarchical power is justified by property rights, as in a corporation, or by the right of representation, as in a political Party or a democratic nation. By force of deeply rooted drives in human nature itself, institutional leadership becomes a breeding ground for power-corruption, dependency, alienation, and spiritual-psychological exploitation. Therefore, at long last, for the first political time – this organizational design abolishes institutional leadership. *No more of that, not in our organization!* We shall leave that particular cause of corruption of the organizational experience behind us once and for all.

We shall replace institutionalized political leadership with organizational arrangements that acknowledge both human nature and the need of members to accomplish their political tasks effectively by working together. In suggesting an alternative to institutionalized leadership, we take into account dependency needs that Lewis Mumford, the eminent historian of cultures, described in the following quote:

> In their impatience, in their despair, people secretly long to cast the burden of their own regeneration upon a savior: a president, a pope, a dictator – vulgar counterparts of a divinity debased or a corruption deified. But such a leader is only the mass of humanity writ small: the incarnation of our resentments, hates, sadisms, or our own cowardices, confusions, and complacencies. – *(Mumford 1973).*

We do not distance ourselves from the mass of humanity in all its negative aspects, but we can take measures to compensate for human deficiencies in designing our organization. Nothing human should be alien to us. Some of us have a lot of natural leadership talent and others little or none at all. During group decision making, some individuals will be more dominant, more skilled in convincing others to support their position and more influential in guiding the process toward their preferred outcome. Each person is unique in his or her natural characteristics, but in our organization charisma will not be *institutionalized*. Leadership in the web-movement will remain spontaneous and natural. Only the dependency of executives on their small group of equals will be institutionalized in this Blueprint: executives are still members of their Affinity Group and dependent of its decisions.

In suggesting an alternative to institutionalized leadership, this blueprint also acknowledges the need for organizations to be effective and efficient in their actions. For example, if the Web Movement runs in elections to governing positions in the community or, hopefully, the country, Some people must be appointed to represent it. Some people must be charged with specific roles because in many situations decisions that apply in a broader scope than the Affinity Group cannot be made on time by all members. All these considerations are present in the following arrangements that do away with institutionalized leadership.

1. All executive roles, without exception, will rotate. No person will hold any leadership, executive, or representative position more than the minimum necessary period – one term. You shall decide how long is one term but take care that no behind is stuck in an executive armchair, ever!
2. Executives and functionaries of the Web will abstain, when in office, from using their positions for participation in the Party's decision-making on matters of "ideology", "party-line" or any of its internal issues. For example, if the Web had a newsletter or a newspaper, contributions of executives would not be preferentially treated for publication. If the Person-Centered Party succeeded in having its representatives elected to national, state, or local political power positions, they could not use their positions as springboards for influencing the Web's internal discussion and decision-making. They could, naturally, have equal access to influence on Web decision-making through their Affinity Groups, just like every other member.
3. The organic-personal character of organizational life will prevail in appointing members to executive and representative positions. The Affinity Group can choose one of its members to apply for any organizational position, if it decides it has a suitable candidate. Candidates from different groups will themselves convene as a small group together for a weekend or, if they decide so, longer. There they can get to know one another, their views, aspirations, plans, skills, etc., and on the basis of that interpersonal data and impressions choose, by consensus or vote, their candidate or candidates for the organization's executive post. If there are many more candidates, the next level of selection will involve those chosen in the first round, in the same direct-interpersonal, open and democratic way.

This arrangement will do away with the corruption-breeding "primary" system, with all its primitive tricks of self-advertisement, self-aggrandizement, scheming and fund-raising for the candidate, spending wads of money, bribing pressure groups for support, and the like. No more lies of the "Public Relations" genre, no more "image-makers" … (The author is best acquainted with conditions in his own country, Israel, but, to the best of his knowledge, the corruption-ridden processes by which political parties elect their leaders are not much different elsewhere in the "Free World"). Person-Centered organization will prevent all those means of corruption in the process of appointing people to power position by making the whole process interpersonal, open and informed directly in small groups. Such setting will best prevent *Psychological* exploitation aimed to bypass critical independent thinking. In politics and in consumer culture, politicians and Ad-men regularly employ psychologically exploitative tactics to influence people. In contrast, a small group of equals would not be fertile ground for manipulative rhetoric.

* * *

That is a complete general outline of the egalitarian, Person-Centered political organization. Now you have read the recipe for how the organization should make coordinated decisions, govern itself, divide authority, and structure the participation of its individual members. You could see in the Blueprint how its structure avoids the traps of corruption by inflammatory, deceitful and divisive rhetoric in influencing the organizational decision-making on personal, material and "ideological" issues. We shall presently offer a detailed description of the actual experience of individuals in the Web-Movement's Affinity Groups, supporting our proposals as we go along with existing know-how and earlier experience.

Reading a recipe cannot replace the actual experience of cooking. However, this recipe has all the ingredients necessary for achieving a position of political power in the community, or even in the country, without compromising your human values and with good chances of preserving your solidarity and affinity with other members. This Blueprint intends, as well, to keep you going and make you feel good about your political experience.

At the very least, this recipe promises to contain the strongest antidotes to the Power Corruption and unrestrained interpersonal conflict that have poisoned the lives of most idealistic and conscientious reformers or revolutionaries, and often resulted in their paving the road to hell with good intentions.

Living experience in a Person-Centered Party

Why choose small groups?

In light of the evaluated experience and knowledge in the area of organizational dynamics, the small group structure should be the best alternative for organizational effectiveness that goes along with democratic decision-making, personal freedom and high quality interpersonal life. This conclusion rests on organizational characteristics such as sharing information and openness in problem solving, as well as in conflict resolution (Bennis, Benne and Chin, 1961; Argyris, 1971; Merry and Allerhand, 1977). The framework of a small group is required to break the vicious cycle of idealization-disappointment-alienation into which many conscientious individuals stumble in modern affluent society.

Some Background, Past and Present

Historically, the small group has been the chosen organizational alternative of person-centered thinkers. In humanistic philosophy it is found in Martin Buber's "living units of relations" (Buber, 1948). In applied behavioral science, it builds on small-group theory, research, and experience (Bradford et al., 1964). In socio-political theory, Erich Fromm (Fromm, 1962), a prominent pioneer in humanistic political psychology, advanced it just before the "New Left" era of the 1960s. Currently, it is advocated and practiced in the U.S. as the framework for making Democracy really work, by groups such as the National Coalition for Dialogue & Deliberation, the Co-Intelligence Institute (Atlee, 2000), and others. Social Activists are becoming increasingly aware that without person-to-person dialogue and deliberation democracy could become empty of human contents. Many social critics claim that Democracy in the rich countries is actually a system by which the ruling elite manipulates most people to alienate them from the political process and make them unable to think of alternatives.

Applied Behavioral Science, though, suggests viable alternatives to organizational life that are more collaborative and less competitive without being less effective. They promote Organizational Development with valid information, open two-way communication and open resolution of conflicts. Behavioral Science has not affected political power systems so far, but alternative ways exist, and we can implement them in a political organization to make it free of power corruption.

The Power Corrupts spell still persists; I do not know of any political Party in the world that is not structured like a pyramid of power. However, among politically active people, a feeling is growing that those who enlist as Party members should become empowered by more means than just being allowed to cast a vote every few years.

If our goal were only to insure equal access of all members to organizational decision-making, with no intent to change the alienated condition of political experience, another arrangement would also be possible. Modern means of communication allow unlimited numbers of people to participate in decision-making by casting their votes by telephone or digitally. Indeed, an effort to "take back our sovereign legislative power" is already under way in the U.S., where the National Institute for Democracy works for a Democracy amendment to the Constitution that would allow citizens to vote on laws of their own making. By this proposal citizens could legislate without having to participate in any interpersonal process other than going through the legal procedures. The Internet can technically be the vehicle of decision-making without direct interpersonal involvement.

Direct individual voting on legislation, or "Government by Polling", would technically serve the values of majority rule, equality in power sharing and participation, better than the existing system of political parties and their representatives. However, without a genuine high-quality process of dialogue and deliberation, public opinion would lack most of what is valued in its wisdom. That value comes from passing one's opinions through the testing ground of human congregation, interrelation, discussion, process, growth and change. Without interpersonal processes, minority opinions or any new and creative ideas would have no chance to be heard and discussed. In the absence of genuine dialogue, decision-making would become the result of computation rather than deliberation, as in public opinion polls. The democratic process would be reduced to counting the hands of isolated and most often alienated people.

It would be technically possible to form small discussion and decision-making groups electronically, in writing or even talking to and seeing one another. If that experience works, people involved in such medium-mediated interpersonal communication could then decide for themselves if and how often they would meet face to face. With further development of visual media, even ones that have developed since I first drafted this Blueprint, video conferences could facilitate live interpersonal interaction and deliberation in small groups.

Some background considerations are due here. The ideals of freedom, social justice, human rights, such as found expression in the American, French or the Socialist revolutions, belonged to people who lived in societies afflicted by political oppression, organized terror, fear, and abysmal destitution. Violence in their world was an inseparable part of political life, like the air they breathed. Some revolutionaries affirmed, in perfect faith, Liberty-Equality-Fraternity but ended on the scaffold, others proclaimed collective ideals but wasted away in concentration camps and forced labor gulags. Some became or were followed in power by tyrants, slave-owners, totalitarian oppressors and genocidal murderers of entire peoples. Most of their former supporters, many millions, became physically their victims, abused in the name of their ideals. We are largely safe from such threats, even that of pestilence or famine. Modern affluent democratic society protects us with its technological means – so let us not forget to count our blessings.

However, our Freedom and our aspirations for Brotherhood and Sisterhood (or as it is now politically *correcter* to say "Siblinghood") – not to mention Equality, which is cheerfully sacrificed on the altar of material affluence – are constantly being spoiled by isolation, alienation, escapism, merciless competition and violence ... Most of us spend our lives in a compulsive, competitive "pursuit of happiness", e.g. the quest for money and cheap thrills. The system offers us a plethora of easy substitutes for a life of freedom and personal independence, political equality, and human relatedness. As the Historian of American Culture Neil Postman put it, "Big Brother is not watching us; we watch him!" Many heads are guillotined pleasantly without separating them from shoulders; heads empty of motives and ideas such as would befit the free spirits and independent minds of persons who take charge of their destiny and the destiny of their society. The American Co-Intelligence Institute, which supports and trains facilitators for small groups of citizens practicing democracy by deliberating issues, introduces itself by quoting Alexander Hamilton in Federalist No. 71: *The deliberative sense of the community should govern.* Now, just imagine what would become of the deliberation process that led the American Founding Fathers to draft their Constitution, if each of them had had a TV set with 54 channels at home? – They would not have had time left for deliberation after consuming all those distractions. Our community, as described by many humanistic social thinkers, consists of willing conformists (Galbraith, 1973; Huxley, 1958; Postman, 1986). The economist J. K. Galbraith wrote:

> *The emancipation of belief requires presumption against all persuasion by the planning system. Such persuasion exists to impose the goals of the technostructure on the individual. The individual who wishes to be free cannot, therefore, accede. He must resist. Anyone who without thought yields to persuasion as to purchases, behavior, or belief, yields something of himself to the purposes of the planning system."* – J. K. Galbraith: *Economics and the Public Purpose*

The "technostructure" system does not touch our physical tissue, it only shortcuts the energy needed for establishing a meaningful dialogue between individuals and their fellows about their political duties and decisions. All this "unfreedom", as Herbert Marcuse, one of the ideological idols of the New Left, coined it – is a condition most of us willingly accept. We are usually not even aware of it.

What steps can we take toward humanization of our individual political experience? – We suggest the small group, as the solid building block of organization, not only as an alternative to built-in organizational corruption caused by institutionalized inequality and structural conflict, but also as an alternative to political alienation, the actual political non-existence of so many people! The human-scaled political structure is suited for establishing meaningful ties with others on political issues and making effective group decisions on those issues. Furthermore, the person-to-person environment is the logical situation for liberation from psychological exploitation by mind-manipulators using mass media and the bullhorns of leadership positions. Based on current knowledge, the small group it is the best setting for supporting individual self-expression and personal growth.

> *The fundamental fact of human existence is neither the individual as such nor the aggregate as such. Each, considered by itself, is a mighty abstraction. The individual is a fact of existence insofar as he steps into a living relation with other individuals. The aggregate is a fact of existence insofar as it is built up of living units of relations. The fundamental fact of human existence is man with man.* – Martin Buber.

To meet the needs of free and self-motivated persons who want to be actively involved in making decisions for socio-political change, the small size of Affinity Groups is necessary for reasons of space and time. You may verify that assertion with your personal experience, beginning with your experiences as a child in a school classroom. Your freedom of self-expression in public was necessarily limited by the need to share with other children the teacher's space, time, and attention. The more people assemble in one communication space, the more individuals must be limited and restrained to make communication possible. Above a certain threshold, a division of roles between speakers and audience becomes necessary, so equality in affecting the decision-making process becomes less and less possible.

For most people, the small group experience would be ridden with interpersonal problems, as is family life, and similarly irreplaceable. However, unlike a family, it would consist of free adults with equal rights who can learn to make decisions, solve problems, deal constructively with conflicts and develop their interpersonal skills for living in harmony with one another. In doing so, help by experienced facilitators can be very important (Luft, 1970; Schein, 1969). With all the "cold" professional objectivity I am capable of, I see no organizational person-centered alternative to the empowerment of small groups, small enough to be a living web of interrelations among equal individuals. To date, validated experience in human behavior offers no better alternative for supporting the values we seek to realize.

THE REVOLUTIONARY MEANING OF PLANTING A PERSON-CENTERED WEB MOVEMENT ON THE RUINS OF POWER-PYRAMIDS

The organizational network of Affinity Groups is not my original contribution. As I already mentioned, the well-known psychoanalyst Erich Fromm popularized, but did not originate the concept, following in the footsteps of thinkers and social movers like Gustav Landauer. They have been considered utopian, because they did not have the benefits of scientific knowledge about interpersonal processes and group-dynamics that we now have. I do not claim credit for that organizational scheme, so I need not be shy about expressing my enthusiasm for it: It could make possible what so far could not be realized – a decent, human, democratic and egalitarian political power organization. Becoming a member of an organization that puts power in the hands of all members at all times, rather than in the hands of top leaders, would be a radical, revolutionary departure from all the unsuccessful earlier attempts. I see it as an opportunity for individuals in our lifetime to participate in the birth of something new in the world.

All radical reformers and leaders of revolutions that have failed or will fail in the future have overturned the power-pyramid only to stabilize it with themselves on top. The suggested web-organization, however, has a good chance of breaking the historical spell of Power Corrupts, because it would demolish the power-pyramid down to the ground level. On its ruins something new, humanly organic and living would have a realistic chance to arise.

The total demolition of the power-pyramid is not *sufficient* to enable the person-centered organization to achieve its goals without compromising its values. However, it is a *necessary* condition for it. In a power-pyramid organization there is no real chance to succeed, because, despite the best intentions of its founders, corruption of democratic-egalitarian values by power is built-in. The division between management and workers, leaders and followers, people with power and people with no real power maintains and perpetuates itself in all political, military, bureaucratic and economic organizations. For them that is a good solution, but for us it is our *problem*. Now, you must face the truth that the organizational solution you are seeking to maintain a democratic, truly egalitarian and effective political organization – cannot be combined with an institutionalized hierarchy of power and stay true to your stated values. In a political party, each member "shares" organizational power as a small share-holder in a giant corporation – but sharing power is an illusion if not an outright deception. However, we can reverse the decision-making order and give a truly equal share of organizational power to each member. We can create something new under the political sun with a built-in counter-mechanism against our natural drive to overpower and control others regardless of the walls of ideological rationalizations we might build around us to justify it.

Our scheme takes the time-honored idea of checks-and-balances some steps further and into the living fabric of a voluntary political organization. And please, bear in mind that the higher the ideals and loftier the goals and stronger the beliefs of idealists in their ideology, their cause, their leaders and themselves – the more corruption manifested in manipulation of others seems logically justified, along with aggression against "deviants" who think differently, violence, and other "means" that justify the "ends". That is the real dynamic of paving the way to hell with good intentions. That is what we *must* avoid by building the logically strongest system of internal checks and balances, signposts and barriers, around the precipices of power-corruption.

As I understand it – and I see no realistic alternative – the very nature of person-centered values leads to a conclusion that their realization in an organization must involve maximum empowerment of each individual by maximal power sharing. Human nature, as well as historical precedents, makes it highly probable that we need no less than a total demolition of the power pyramid. It's either that, or the organization becomes yet another conflict arena in which, behind an ideological veneer, individual chiefs and their followers compete for power. They try to dominate by climbing over each other's backs, more like rivals or enemies rather than persons working together as brothers/sisters for their common goals.

So let us pause for a minute and contemplate the meaning of the Person-Centered Web concept in the 21st century and this millennium. I believe that anyone who manages to find her or his way to a political organization structured as a web of small Affinity Groups that make decisions for the whole organization will be participating in a completely new political experience. In the frame of mind of a humanist such as our hypothetical client or reader – this Blueprint offers him or her participation in the birth of something new and liberating in the world.

PERSON-CENTERED POLITICAL ORGANIZATION FOR WHAT?

"Participation in the birth of something new in the world" sounds exciting – but for what political purposes? – For *your* purposes, of course. The author, as your organizational consultant, has offered an alternative for those of you who reject the presently existing political party experience as inadequate or incompatible with your values. Now readers can follow this Blueprint in reaching their own goals, in their own time and place. My responsibility is to ensure that you can experience a true democratic, person-centered *quality of life* in your organization. For that goal, we will now go into precise and even minor details, including everything that may help avoid problems for those who would move from this "prescription" to real life.

The quality of organizational life is something that is difficult to cheat on or have illusions about. People who experience it feel it. We must ensure that the organizational corruption we avoided by abolishing the pyramid of power and arranging for decisions to flow from all member-groups does not infect the group itself with inefficient, unequal, unfair, and undemocratic communication and behavior patterns.

Power-pyramids attract people with stronger power and competitive drives and fewer scruples. They discourage more sensitive, independent, and conscientious persons, who are neither naturally aggressive nor willing followers of leaders and crowds. Our suggestions aim at creating such an organizational climate in the web-organization that would be suited for the latter types and discourage the more conflicted on issues of power and control of others.

In contrast to all our predecessors, today we possess sources of practical knowledge about interpersonal dynamics that make it possible to structure decision-making processes differently, in ways that do not cause the usual burnout afflicting sensitive and conscientious people in hierarchical and conflict ridden organizations. The alternative ways include open resolution of conflicts, open communication and, most importantly, including the group's quality of life itself as a regular item on its agenda. Upon suggesting these alternative procedures, we may responsibly claim that today we know more about how to narrow the gap between good intentions and organizational reality than we have ever known before.

DEDICATION: I dedicate this section to Betty Doerr and Vicki Legion, two women who in their youth joined the American radical "Movement" (nowadays referred to as the "New Left") of the 1960s and early 1970s.

They wrote the following "Letter to the Movement" for its periodical "Liberation". Since reading their article, I have had those two women and their experience on my mind, seeking to find an alternative way of forming a "Movement" that will ensure that what they and many thousands of others experienced would not happen again.

> The women's movement experience pushed us into some fruitful struggling against our competitive upbringing, but the old ways are hard dying. Correct-lining, snap judgments and labeling make us lose the exploration of real differences in a haze of rhetoric, personal attack and counterattack. When we're preoccupied with our fear of being labeled, our ability to think critically gets suspended.
>
> Right/wrong thinking impedes critical thinking and creativity. I am sad at how often I have seen this dynamic play itself out in discussions. Marx, or Third World revolutionaries, or the Panthers or some other authority is defined as "Right". Anyone who questions what the authority says is at best "wrong" and at worst "counterrevolutionary". The discussion degenerates into a biblical exegesis, with different sides swapping quotes and impressions. Facts and experiences that don't fit "the line" are ignored. Real differences are obscured in barrages of rhetoric, while new events are jammed into old categories. So much for our ability to respond creatively to changing conditions. – *Betty Doerr and Vicki Legion, "Letter to a Movement"*, Liberation, July-August 1974.

The above text says it all. No more of that!

LIFE, REGULATIONS, AND ORGANIZATION: BASIC CONSIDERATIONS

When we approach organizational rules and regulations, we have to keep in mind some basic considerations regarding the interrelation of individual freedom, interpersonal communication, and the public interest. By rules and regulations, we mean all that governs and regulates conduct in institutions such as states, corporations, schools, even families: institutional norms, contracts, laws, by-laws, in short – all that limits free interaction between individuals.

Rules and regulations can be compared to roads and trails that people open in the territory of their living environment in order to avoid bumping into or running over one another. On both sides of those trails there are ravines that are all too easy to stumble into: hierarchy on the right and anarchy on the left.

Watch out on your Left:

Anarchism and anarchy can be very attractive to people who value their personal freedom above all. That attractiveness lasts as long as they do not try to practice it in large numbers. Knowing many anarchistic spirits from personal experience and having myself similar sentiments, I believe that many well-intentioned rebellious people will not oppose the organizational program suggested here. Anarchism as a political strategy is, for conscientious people, a default option in a world in which they do not see better alternatives. Just recently, I read a message from one of the leaders of the British radical scene, in which he clearly admitted "we don't know how to organize effectively" and justified his suggestion that we'd be better off not trying. Here, I believe, is the way people like him might consider trying.

Anarchy is great and sounds great in art and music, for example, at rock concerts. On stage, anarchy is an artistic illusion created by much hard, well-disciplined work in rehearsals. Below the stage-level, it could quickly become a disaster area, were there no regulations and no authorities to enforce them: sell tickets, control the entrance, and generally take care that the masses of young anarchistic spirits will not be trampled on or suffocated in their crowd.

An anarchistic state with no effective police force would become more violent than a totalitarian police state, because when all limitations on free interpersonal interaction are suspended, criminals have a free hand to attack and exploit ordinary citizens. Unlimited and unregulated freedom is an invitation to act out the instinctive violence in human nature (think of the anarchistic principle in relation to the free sale of weapons). Therefore anarchy is necessarily ineffective as a strategy to create and maintain a safe and open society. The bulk of normal humanity fears anarchy and tries to escape it as quickly as it can. Look back on the last decades: Hippies have been replaced by Yuppies. The French overwhelmingly supported the authoritarian de Gaulle when threatened by the anarchistic student "revolt" of 1968. In that revolt, the most celebrated (by the media, how else) leader was Daniel Cohn-Bendit (then called Dany le Rouge or Danny the Red), who specifically opposed formal organization. Over the years, he became more organizationally "square" and was even elected to the German Parliament (Bundestag). One of the similarly celebrated figures in the U.S. at the time was Abbie Hoffman. His fabled bestseller "*Revolution for the Hell of It*", written under the nom de plume "Free", inspired the masses (mostly of adolescents) with wishful-thinking "observations" such as "The stable middle-class home is falling apart". He himself ultimately became, predictably, a stable middle-class home type, an insurance agent as I heard. Thc important political fact of life remains the victory of Richard Nixon in the 1972 presidential elections in all states but one, and the emergence of the "moral majority" in the U.S. It must have occurred, at least to a certain extent, as a backlash against the anarchistic "counterculture", of "flower-children" who left their cultural mark on the "New Left" of the 1960s. Their anarchistic ideology swept America with provocative slogans such as "Screw the System".

Those who resist any organizational rules and regulations would, first, never be able to organize. Therefore, they would indeed be free only of means to control their destiny; not free from living for the rest of their and their children's lives under the social system or regime they so much wish to change. Or, they could become free riders on the system's back, allowed to sing and dance, watch anarchy on TV and go around free to grumble, protest and demonstrate in the system's public gardens as long as they do not cross the barriers put up by the police.

Watch out on your right:

On the right-hand side of regulated roads there lie the pitfalls of hierarchy leading first to corruption of person-centered egalitarian-democratic values and then, further down, to authoritarianism. Still further down the revolutionary road we find Animal Farm types of tyranny. Therefore, in order to avoid pitfalls on the Right, we need such rules and regulations that, on the one hand, would ensure security and personal freedom, and on the other hand grant conditions for effective decision-making. Our rules and regulations need to satisfy the free-spirited but not irresponsible individual members. For that, they must prevent deterioration to power relationships while maintaining satisfactory relationships among equals and leave enough space for free activity, spontaneity and creativity. Rules and regulations need to assist personal freedom rather than hinder it; they need to be at a *minimal* level but *not below it*.

In suggesting rules and regulations for life in the Affinity Group, my stand at the point of departure is that the meaningful difference between any good and bad system, be it as big as a state or as small as a family, is not between having rules and regulations and being free of any rules and regulations. The difference between hope and despair, freedom and oppression, equality and exploitation lies in the difference between good laws and regulations well administered; and bad laws and regulations or any laws and regulations poorly administered, resulting in oppression, misery, confusion and conflict.

To sum it up: No Organization, so far, has led to Liberation – sad but true. However, the fact of political life is **No Liberation without Organization**. – As long as well-intentioned and decent people do not learn how to organize effectively to gain political power without compromising their values of equality in power-sharing – the free spirits who wish to change political reality are destined to live powerlessly in a world of *inequality* where if not they some other people will suffer from domination, exploitation, or oppression.

RULES AND REGULATIONS ARE LIKE RECIPES; WE DO THE COOKING

Another point regarding rules and regulations is important to keep in mind. They are human inventions that become, like signposts, part of our social environment. However, human life and behavior can never be completely regulated, signposts can forever be misunderstood or ignored and could never regulate every aspect of human life. Even in total institutions, such as prisons or concentration camps, prisoners have some space for behaving according to their inner self-regulation systems, for better or worse. The success of a society or an organization is overwhelmingly dependent on the rules governing it, but never independent of people's will and ability to follow, interpret, and apply the rules in any new situation in an ever-changing reality. Organizational rules and regulations are necessary but never sufficient.

The United States has a Constitution, and it is impossible to imagine it could survive as a nation without it. Nevertheless, even such a magnificent constitution must be interpreted and amended if needed, and could be distorted and even emptied of meaning. All religions have rules, and yet their leaders must do the interpretation, change, and adaptation of their regulations, however divine they may or may not be. Democratic laws and procedures may formally regulate the country, but most citizens may lack a democratic education, mentality and skills.

Laws and regulations serve as means to translate values into patterns of living. In any case, rules in themselves would not insure the realization of any value. Unless one sees solitude as his or her supreme value, regardless of how attractive the values, absence of rules would result in conflict that could lead only to either disintegration or to realization of the dominant patterns by force.

The power of any social contract is dependent on the willingness of people to uphold and the ability of society to enforce it. Since the Affinity Group of the organizational Web-Movement is meant to be a voluntary association of free individuals, nobody will be able to enforce anything on it. The effectiveness of its rules and regulations would depend only on the willingness and ability of group members to abide by them. We shall presently suggest the best rules and regulations for the group process we know of today. As your organizational consultant, I have chosen them from T-group ("T" for training) theory and experience in interpersonal skills development. They would be like a recipe for you. The results will depend on your "cooking" skills. In practice, you have all the freedom you need to change the recipe to suit your needs, change ingredients, and instead use different ones to suit your taste.

* * *

EQUALITY AND POWER-SHARING IN THE PROCESS OF DECISION-MAKING

In contrast to all known political organizations, the egalitarian Web gives its Affinity Groups the right and power to make decisions for the whole movement on a regular basis. Now we need to suggest to individuals how to use that power in the best way and not waste it. Life in a political group is not just socializing. It is work. Our work is making decisions for our own group and for the entire organization, and carrying them out. If we do not make decisions, or make decisions and do nothing to implement them, the group will become a social club or a discussion club. For members who want to make a political difference in society, such a group would lose its purpose for being.

Democratic decision-making is a conscious human endeavor. It requires proper physical conditions for enabling people to communicate and discuss their issues, and then make their decision by an accepted procedure. That was so even in the Athenian democracy. The necessary but limited physical resource for democratic decision-making is *time*: time to respond, time to influence, time to argue, time to listen, time to think, to answer, to make up one's mind, etc.

The *quality of life* in decision-making is largely a function of time-sharing and time-using. The lower the quality of life in decision-making, the more aggressiveness you can feel in people's fighting for time: shouting, cutting each other off, trying to seize the greatest possible amount of time. If they snatch the mike from each other, you can see the physical character of such aggressive behavior more distinctly. We must therefore find arrangements that would ensure maximum quality of democratic life in sharing the precious common resource for decision-making: *Time*.

In light of the physical constraints of time, and in light of your needs and values, you may evaluate the following rules for conducting the regular meetings of Affinity Groups. This "recipe" will enable you to treat one another with experience that is truly democratic, not putrefied by incompetence and not corrupted by power. The solution to our problem of high-quality democratic decision-making is called an "**Egalitarian Group Working Process**".

Think of the small Affinity Group as the way to humanize organizational *space*. Think of the Egalitarian Group Working Process as a way to humanize organizational *time*.

Egalitarian Group Working Process

1. **Appointment or election of a chairperson.**
2. **Setting the time limit for the decision-making process.**
3. **Ratification of the Agenda.**
4. **Division of the group's time (as set in No. 2.) among agenda items.**
5. **Appointment of a "Time Keeper" who reminds speakers, if needed, that the time agreed upon is over or about to end.**
6. **Discussion and decision on each of the agenda items, within the time limit decided upon beforehand (No. 4).**
7. **With each agenda item, displaying the decision made in writing, including assignment of people responsible for carrying it out.**
8. **Feedback.**

This is the "recipe" of rules for decision-making in the Affinity Group. We know that people do not like to be ruled and regulated. Perhaps it would be more pleasant if we referred to the **Egalitarian Group Working Process** as "Rules of the Game". However, the truth is that it is not a game. That is our political life in its most significant manifestation. Changes, improvements, adaptations of the process, would of course be possible and would be natural. No professional solution based on a scientific approach claims perfection or resists improvement; no recipe can replace actual cooking.

This Egalitarian Group Working Process is the best I know of today; and now, having presented it, I need to explain, clarify and justify the inclusion of its particular elements.

STEP 1: APPOINTMENT OR ELECTION OF A CHAIRPERSON

The "chairperson" is the person authorized by the group for managing the shared working time according to the group's decisions, dividing and apportioning time among members and agenda items. Why do we need a formally appointed chairperson? Why is it a good idea to make one person "more equal", and why should he or she be more empowered than others? – Well, that chairperson would have much responsibility going along with the authority he or she would have. That person could exercise all the authority she or he has, but only in front of the entire group, nowhere else. The most obvious reason for having a chairperson is something you can sense in the processes of decision-making used by other groups. In such a rare instance, we can follow the good example of parliamentary procedures. Just imagine what would happen if the discussion and decision-making processes of political assemblies, congresses and parliaments were not conducted according to strict procedures imposed by the speaker, the chairperson.

If the number of people involved is not greater than six and all of them are exceptionally skilled in interpersonal communication, they could perhaps do without a chairperson. Perhaps they could make decisions with no formal structure, freely and spontaneously like friends over a cup of coffee, with no chairperson or any formally assigned roles. However, even in a dialogue between two persons, the freedom of each to use time for presenting, substantiating or defending his or her position is limited by the very presence of the other. Time must be shared fairly for people to feel good about it. In reality, only if each of the participants is exceptionally gifted in the art of interpersonal communication can they get along well without an appointed chairperson or other rules and regulations. If, for example, even one fellow among them is a well meaning bore, that would become hard or impossible.

By skills of interpersonal communication, often referred to as "the Art of interpersonal relationship", I mean the most important skills for living that schools seldom teach. To reach a satisfactory level of mutual understanding and of collaboration for common goals, without an institutionalized hierarchy and without degenerating into power-corruption, you would need to operate on a much higher level of interpersonal competence without a coordinator than when there is one. With the support of good agreements on the process of decision-making, people would develop their skills of interaction naturally, as most of us learn from experience. To facilitate that, the Egalitarian Working Group Process contains Feedback, an item specifically added to improve a group's level of interpersonal relations in decision-making and collaboration in implementation of the decisions made.

With that, regardless of your political involvement in the Web-Movement, it is best to learn the skills of interpersonal behavior by attending specific learning experiences in Group Dynamics guided by professional trainers. In a setting of small groups in which the interpersonal process "here and now" is the subject of learning, participants learn skills from their own life experience. Such learning is justly called "personal growth". Carl Rogers, the eminent humanistic psychologist and psychotherapist, referred to Encounter Groups in Group Dynamics as "*perhaps the most significant social invention of the century*" (Rogers, 1970). In my personal experience, the T-Group has been my most important and rewarding personal-growth experience. It is also the most egalitarian, participatory, non-authoritarian learning method.

Therefore, if your process of decision-making in a group is to be free, unstructured and unregulated, you will soon feel what in Group Dynamics training is called "a pinch". This is the moment people feel that the atmosphere becomes tense, dense or heavy; or realize that it becomes difficult to contribute to a discussion without forcing one's ideas on others; or that the discussion moves around and around without any progress in going anywhere; or that people occasionally lose patience, erupt, block one another, do not listen, etc. Then it should be understood that some formal procedures for conducting a meeting must be agreed upon and followed. The formal agreement of the group on its procedures will serve as a means for regulating how and by whom and how much of the group's working time should be used. The accepted general rule in working groups is, "*Agreement on Process should Precede Agreement on Contents*".

Chances are you would need a chairperson and a formal procedure in decision-making. At the same time, egalitarian values and people's individual well-being require a sensitive application of the rules. The idea should be that the more members rotate the chairperson job among them the better. Each chairperson of a meeting should think of the job as if he or she were the treasurer and the group working time the cash given him or her for safekeeping. The chairperson has to see to it that time is not squandered or appropriated by unauthorized persons. The group's time is a precious asset that belongs to all. It must be shared in fairness.

STEP 2: SETTING THE TIME LIMIT FOR THE DECISION-MAKING PROCESS.

All we need is that the chairperson proposes when the decision-making session should be ended, and the group makes the decision on that time. This procedure is natural and innocent enough; it could be applied in any session of any group that makes decisions. But readers who, like this author, have spent hundreds of hours of the best years of their lives in boring, tedious, tense and irritating sessions of committees or teams have had a different experience more often than not: The top-job holder comes, announces the agenda and begins to talk right away. Nobody knows when exactly this is going to be over, except for the comforting notion that at some not-too-distant time in the future there is going to be a coffee break and, sometime later, there is going to be an end to it and one will be free to go home. If the participants care and have a real personal stake in what is being decided, such meetings could be compared to a ball game in which the players do not know when the whistle signaling the end of the game is going to be sounded, and how much longer they need to play to win. Such players would not know for how long to plan their strategy, save their energy, and what is going to happen next; and so they would become exhausted and aggressive, and kick at each other's shins.

Democratic decision-making is an inherently competitive situation. In the absence of clear rules governing time, when the issue becomes hot the discussion heats up. Everyone is trying to "score" the decision, so they keep the "ball" (the floor) as long as they can to themselves. Often the result remains zero: zero decisions, zero positive energy left, and zero good will to go on like that next time.

In such conditions the stage is set for the more energetic (that sometimes means "brutal') – less democratic persons, usually natural manipulators of people, to become the real makers and movers of decisions. Decisions, if any, will be made by one or several persons, either in the last moments of the meeting using strong pressure and with total exhaustion of all who have resisted, or if after the session a few stronger players clinch a deal among themselves.

No more of that! – The shared decision-making process, in contrast, gives the group full control over the use of its time. Therefore, you must decide (explicitly agree and put in writing) when the time for making the decision begins and when it will end. Efficiency, even in machines, means work done per unit of time.

If the group takes full responsibility and full control over the use of its time for doing its work, it could use and allocate its energy well and accomplish its task. That accomplishment will make participants feel good: feel that the "game" they have played was decent and fair; that they could all speak their mind and be heard. Everyone should feel they had an equal opportunity in decision-making, so they would "own" the decisions made as theirs, even when they themselves held a minority opinion on a particular issue.

STEP 3: RATIFICATION OF THE AGENDA BY THE GROUP

Display the agenda for the group meeting written on a board or flip-chart with items numbered according to urgency. After setting the time frame for decision-making, the next thing to do is to agree on the agenda. That stage in the decision-making process is necessary, because you need to minimize the possibility that some members would have to take part in the discussion feeling that the issue is not worth it, or the group has not been sufficiently prepared for making a decision. If you do not ratify the agenda first, individuals may become frustrated, believing that other topics are more important and urgent; or that their important issue has again been left off the group's agenda. Situations, in which some individuals would not be happy with the issue the group chose to discuss, cannot be entirely avoided, but they will occur less frequently and be easier to bear if each person has an equal opportunity to set the agenda before the group starts working on it.

Think of making decisions as deciding, "*What do we do next*". Think of ratifying the agenda as deciding, "*Where do we go next*". Whoever has the power to decide where everybody is going next has a decisive organizational power. That power we want to share equally, so we put it in the hands of every individual in the group by prior ratification of the agenda. Your values of equality in power sharing demand that no human "bulldozer" should be able to make decisions without first getting an OK from the group for putting them on its agenda.

Further, efficiency in decision-making demands that we be very conscious of time constraints. Therefore, the Egalitarian Group Working Process requires that agenda ratification will be settled quickly. The organizational structure of the Web would make the most of the Affinity Group agenda to contain the movement's political items. Groups will have their own agenda too. All constraints notwithstanding, we strongly suggest that the principle of ratifying the agenda first be followed. Individuals at this stage of the group's work would be able to motion for adding items to the agenda or omitting items for that session.

The ratification-of-agenda stage should be brief, with no discussion permitted. Persons suggesting a change in the presented agenda could explain their suggestion in one or two sentences, with no time for others to raise objections. The group will decide whether to admit or reject the change there and then, by consensus or majority vote.

In the regular work of decision-making groups, it is advisable that the first item on the agenda should be a report by those who were charged with implementing previously made decisions. This is a requirement of effectiveness in work. It will become more time-effective if the reports are prepared in writing and handed to members ahead of time. When we reach that stage (no. 6) in group work, I shall delineate in more detail what can be built into the decision-making process to make decisions effective in terms of making a political difference in the social environment.

STEP 4: DIVISION OF WORKING TIME AMONG AGENDA ITEMS

This particular item of the Egalitarian Group Working Process would make a big difference for everyone who has ever participated in group meetings, sessions, committees, forums, etc. It requires that, prior to the beginning of work on the agenda, the group decides how much of its total working time will be dedicated to each of the items. The best way to go over this part of the process is the clearest one: write down the agenda on a board or a flip-chart for all to see and write down next to each item how long you will work on it before making a decision on it and moving to the next item.

I see this step in the process as absolutely necessary for the same reasons that made us decide when to start and when to finish. The actual decision-making process is a cycle of the group's life that focuses on each issue: introduction, discussion, suggestions for resolution, decision (by consensus or voting), and putting on the record for implementation. The need to control the precious resource – time – that applies to the whole session applies to each such cycle. That requires that when opening the process of deliberation on an item, we need to be agreed on how long it could take of our time to make that decision. By structuring our working time to be portioned among the agenda items, we ensure that we are not 'sucked' into one item and left with no time to take care of others. That way we provide for meeting our goals: efficiency in work, equality in time-sharing, and generating good feelings that come with high quality of organizational life.

STEP 5: APPOINTMENT OF A "TIMEKEEPER" TO REMIND SPEAKERS, WHEN NEEDED, THAT THE ALLOTTED TIME IS OVER OR ALMOST OVER

I see this suggestion as optional. Perhaps you could use the time wisely and divide it fairly without the services of a "time-keeper". In any event, the chairperson can use the assistance of another person who would sit with watch in hand and concentrate on carrying out the decisions the group has made about its use of time. If there is a need to limit a speaker's time, the Timekeeper will have the duty and the authority to tell speakers things like "you have one minute to finish" or "your time is over"...

The basic datum that prompts me to suggest the Timekeeper function is that democratic groups have tremendous psychological difficulty to deal openly with problems of individual use – and misuse – of time. Much good will and many excellent ideas get lost forever because of that little thorn in the group's flesh: the difficulty to share time effectively and fairly among individuals, in a way that would not hurt the feelings of many sincere people whose egos are much more sensitive than their biological clocks. It is difficult to overstate the extent to which practical skills in democratic decision-making are dependent on time and on sound procedures to cope with conflicts inherent in sharing time.

Therefore, we suggest that the most important principle in determining whether or not to appoint a Timekeeper should be that *time is what is actu-*

ally shared in power-sharing during decision-making. Therefore, the group has to be very careful, open, and determined in maintaining full control over its time, whatever it takes, including a Timekeeper.

STEP 6: DISCUSSION AND DECISION ON EACH OF THE AGENDA ITEMS WITHIN THE AGREED-ON TIME-SPAN

When the time allotted for discussion of an agenda item nears its end, the chairperson or the Timekeeper should inform the group that the time for arguing is over, and a time for decision-making has come. From that moment on there is no more time for persuasion, explanation, clarification, or any form of trying to influence someone else. From then on, time is dedicated only to exact formulation or wording of the proposed decisions to be made.

Additionally, it is strongly recommended that the proposed decisions should be written down and displayed clearly for all to see. Then you'd be ready to vote or to reach a consensus.

In reaching for consensus, make sure that the feeling of general consensus is not illusory or superficial. A group member may push for consensus saying "OK, we're all agreed", whereas in reality some members are not in agreement. They may simply think that under the circumstances there is no chance their voice would be heard or understood, so why bother. Consensus is not the same thing as unanimity. Preferably it could be a situation in which not all participants agree on the proposal as it is, but feel that they had a fair opportunity to voice their opinion in the discussion and the others did listened to them. They accept that they have not persuaded the majority of the group and therefore choose to join the consensus.

* * *

At this point, you might feel that we have gone into too much detail and lost touch with the broader context. So let us take a rest from the details and focus again on the broader horizon of relationships between organizational rules-and-regulations and life. That relationship is like having maps to guide us in the territory. It is relatively easy to prove that the conceptual maps that have in the past guided people in the political organization territory toward human decency, equality, efficiency and inner freedom, were wrong, very wrong in face of human reality. People who espoused such values simply could not reach their destinations. I believe that this Blueprint, as a map of human reality, is correct enough. With it, you can reach your destination and not sail your organizational vessel onto a reef. However, it is equally easy to see that no map can cover all of the territory with all its intricacies and human manifold moods, passions, thinking and behavior. **The Map is Not the Territory**; the recipe is not the food. Movement in the territory depends on the navigator, not only on the map.

Kurt Levin, considered the founding father of Applied Behavioral Science and of "Group Dynamics" (he coined the term), suggested the formula *Behavior = Personality + Environment*. Our rules and regulations, like any rules-of-the-game, constitution or law, are factors in the environment. They can have a tremendous impact on behavior. However, the actual behavior of people in Affinity Groups, as anywhere, would also depend on the individual personality. This has been a disclaimer in the context of assessing your level of trust in the Egalitarian Group Working Process, when you know enough to begin evaluating it.

Having made this disclaimer, much is left to be claimed about applying this process in the group's life. Navigating your way with this map, you can avoid shoals and treacherous winds and currents you would sail into otherwise. Let us review the process so far and see how the map would make it extremely difficult for a group to fail in reaching decisions and turn into a mere discussion group or social club. Following the stages of the process one by one, the group will have to become aware that time is limited and that its work should end at a certain time. That awareness would work for effectiveness in using time and impress on members the difference between their task as a group with *work* to do, and that of any informal gathering. Then the Egalitarian Group Working Process will encourage you to ratify your agenda openly and reach quick agreement on it. That would help people "own" the agenda and reduce the disappointment of those who raised issues for deliberation and decision, and the group has not accepted their issues as items on the agenda for that meeting. Then you would have to reach agreement on when to start and finish each working assignment (each item on the agenda), and that could increase members' awareness that they have an assignment to do and complete. People in the group will be guided by the working process to end drawn-out discussion when the time they decided upon is up. They would find it difficult to forget or disregard their rules, because the chairperson and the timekeeper will be responsible for keeping the group on schedule. Then, following the process, they will *have to* make decisions!

* * *

End of detour, back to the next stage of the Egalitarian Group Working Process. It is natural that when the time for discussion of an agenda item runs out, members would want to add argumentation, clarify points, and press for acceptance of their opinion beyond the time limit. It would be natural that members would manipulate others one way or another, consciously or less consciously, hoping to gain more time and more attention for themselves. However, a procedure that excludes argumentation and persuasion at this stage would not allow anyone to influence others beyond the set limits. The process – let us hope that a competent chairperson and timekeeper are responsible for it – will allow them to focus the energy that motivates them to influence the decision-making only on formulating the propositions to be decided upon. Then the group will choose one proposition by consensus or majority vote.

Adherence to the Egalitarian Decision-making Process at this stage will introduce a small "revolution" in the life-experience of most working groups, committees, etc, as we have known them. The familiar situation in which people's interest flares up around some topic, often in inverse proportion to its significance, to the point that they forget all the rest until their time and energy are spent – that experience will become very unlikely to occur.

STEP 7: DISPLAY IN WRITING THE DECISION MADE AND THE NAMES OF THOSE RESPONSIBLE FOR CARRYING IT OUT.

In going through the stages of the process so far, we took care that the group *works*, that is makes decisions. Now is the time to take care that it will be good work, that the decisions you made are not left on paper but implemented in the real world. The greatest danger, according to the accumulated experience at our disposition, is that the decisions would be just verbal formulations with a life span stretching between the group's decision and the group's protocol records. There the decisions would simply fade into thin air without ever becoming action in reality. In light of past experience, it is difficult to overestimate that danger even when people have the best intentions, are very sophisticated and highly skilled in interpersonal communication including decision-making.

The core of that problem is not in disharmony among people, not even in lack of good correspondence between people and the demands of time. The problem arises from the very foundations of perception and orientation. The lack of correspondence concerns words and things, concepts and the reality they are about, the cognitive Map and the Territory. Step 7 of the Egalitarian Decision-making Process that requires you to specify loud and clear who is responsible for carrying out the group decision, is this Blueprint's reminder to avoid that problem.

WATCH OUT FOR THE PITFALLS OF OVER-ABSTRACTION (LOSING TOUCH WITH REALITY)

> *"I have sworn upon the altar of God almighty eternal hostility towards all forms of tyranny over the minds of man." – Thomas Jefferson*

Here the problem arises from the tendency to over-abstraction ingrained in the human condition. It is a given in all cultures that we tend to regard the concepts that populate our inner space, the mind, as if they were things in external physical reality, the terrain. The first famous example that comes to mind is John Kennedy's saying in his inaugural address "*Do not ask what your country can do for you – ask what you can do for your country*". "You" is clear enough, but "Your Country" is a huge abstraction, not a concrete Thing. "Your Government" is less abstract, more close to the ground of reality, because it makes decisions for the whole country. So the meaning of that phrase is more like *"Do not ask what your Government can do for you – ask what you can do for your Government"* ... Meaningless abstract language can easily find its way into decision-making, but it need not! Some conceptual systems, like politics, including radical politics, use such language a lot and often do nothing else; other conceptual systems, like natural science, do it much less. Our political predecessors struggled with abstract concepts, piled abstractions up into monstrous "ideologies", fought over concepts, killed for concepts, very often not knowing what, if anything, they were thinking and talking *about* in the Territory.

THE TRAGEDY OF ABSTRACT-MINDEDNESS: A PERSONAL CASE STUDY

When I was studying in the U.S. in the 1970s, I was eager to find out whether there were political groups there that were organized differently, more along the lines suggested here. Looking for organizational models that could replace a political Party, I studied Applied Behavioral Science (Organization Development – OD), which was a predominantly American branch of behavioral science, and I naturally wanted to know whether it had been applied anywhere in a political organization.

And indeed, I found one such group that, judging by its written materials, appeared to be more humanistic, sane, and realistic than any political organization I had ever known or heard of. It was called Movement for a New Society (MNS). Their writings stated that they were committed to actualize among themselves, Here-and-Now, the values of living in the new society they visualized for the future. The term "Here-and-Now" belongs to the terminology of Group Dynamics in groups for experiential learning of interpersonal communication skills. There were more indications of the influence of OD on that movement, like the value they saw in open resolution of conflicts and in conscious regard for people's feelings, as well as the terms "*personal growth*" and "*a climate of trust*". They had written down the words that so closely corresponded to my own conviction then as now: "*There can be no radical change without radically changing our own behavior*".

Century and Millennium have changed, and I still have not heard of any political party or movement whose true believers would not feel threatened by that idea, "*There can be no radical change without radically changing our own behavior*". MNS was genuinely radical, different. Organizationally it was made of some small groups around some big universities and was decentralized like this Blueprint suggests. I took part, as an observer, in one of their meetings that was about formulating a position-paper, or as they call it in Party politics, a "Platform". Here is an excerpt from the draft they discussed:

> "We believe that the present exploitative economic system – Capitalism – is a major barrier toward creating a just society capable of meeting human needs."... "We believe that a democratic socialistic society is crucial to ridding ourselves of the irrationality and dehumanization of Capitalism."

The discussion was heavy. Tension, controlled anger, impatience and frustration, could be felt in the participants' tone and body language. It dragged on, however, on the highest level of abstraction, flaunting "big" abstract words: socialism, capitalism, democracy. People behaved themselves very well and tried to listen more than I had ever known in political party meetings before. They worked very hard, but some of the speakers were "heavies", actually boring, and lost the attention of others. They seemed mesmerized by their own rhetoric, losing any sense of what was going on outside their own minds in the "here-and-now".

To me, the most obvious thing in that meeting was that nobody asked practical questions, such as, why do we need to agree on those formulations right now? Why do we need to decide now whether capitalism is or is not a "major barrier" to creating a "just society"? What are we going to do about it tomorrow and in the following month or so, and what, in real life, is meant by ridding ourselves of the irrationality and dehumanization of Capitalism?

They behaved like sleepwalkers, enveloped in the web of their verbal images without questioning what it actually meant for them then and there. The session ended with the following text, on which consensus was quickly and easily reached:

> The terms racism, sexism, classicism, hetero-sexism, and ageism should be available in some form in our literature for those who are struggling with these terms.

Agreement, like the quick consensus reached in that case, is one of the great payoffs of abstract-mindedness. It does not imply any action, so why not agree? The above is a "classical" example of the intellectual fault that enables "*tyranny over the minds of men*" to be so omnipresent and settle so easily. People invent terms (words, verbal expressions or other symbolism) for designating something in reality (racial relations, economic realities, etc.). Then they are "struggling with terms" rather than struggling to find solutions for the issues they face in reality.

The Movement for a New Society did not take off, the ideological flames died down when the fuel was exhausted and left members with no energy to move on. Human energy needs the fuel of success in reaching one's goals, which can be achieved only in working together in reality Here-and-Now. The MNS people knew that there could be no radical change without radically changing their own behavior, but their "ideological" behavior was unworldly. In the crucial area of perceiving, conceptualizing, and acting in reality they were no different from their well-meaning predecessors who had been consumed by their own ideological fires. In the interconnected reality of themselves, social reality, and the concepts they used to give meaning to their reality, the New Left was no different from the Old Left. That – I firmly believe – was their undoing, not any external forces acting on them. At least, as far as my political associates and I are concerned, we must make a promise: NO MORE OF THAT.

* * *

Under a separate title I intend to publish a self-help manual for **Liberation from Psychological Exploitation**, of which over-abstraction is an essential ingredient. Here, within the framework of the Egalitarian Group Working Process, I have chosen the suggested procedures to serve as pegs driven into the ground of reality, tying-down the group lest it soars upward, borne aloft by windy rhetoric and lose contact with the ground. One such procedure is that next to each decision taken, formulated in writing and displayed; it would be written who is assigned to implement it, how soon it must be accomplished, and using what means in case the group's resources are needed.

Each decision made has to be a synopsis of an action-plan, as clear as possible in terms of people, resources, area and time. If it is not so, the decision will be like a map-exercise: a certain point on the map is chosen as the destination but no steps are actually taken to move there in the Territory.

Even in non-political organizations, most group decisions end up in the book of protocols or in general declarations; in political organizations even more so. If you ever listen to speeches of candidates, read political platforms and programs, and ask yourself, "What would they actually do if elected to that office?" you'd seldom find any answers. The speeches are generally abstract generalizations constructed of attractive claims for our side and hostile, negative denunciations of the opponents. "The Party will strive to… act for… develop, ensure, provide… " – nothing, or almost nothing that can be understood as a commitment to do something specific in a specific period of time. That is the character of political rhetoric. That is why politicians love to write those programmatic "Platforms" in abstract terms, in contrast to the concrete language they use when they make real decisions, like who is going to take what position of power, what place on the Party list of candidates, etc. Then their words become sharp and aggressive, or bone-dry and punctilious like the language of formal legal documents. The separation of word and deed is the bread and butter of politics. In contrast, our contract demands we leave that practice behind. It is a narcotic drug for many well-meaning idealists, and therefore we must resolve NO MORE OF THAT. It is necessary that our decision-making should not soar on gusts of hot air into the upper spheres of abstraction, because, at best, it would be self-deception or else deception in general. In a group that is relatively open and honest in its internal discourse, the gap between words and deeds would cause demoralization. If a group cannot find ways to bridge that gap, it will lose its "raison d'être".

Another element of the group working process designed for narrowing the gap between words and deeds, intentions and results would normally be the procedure of putting on the agenda as the first item a report on implementation of decisions made in previous meetings. We must avoid wasting our time and energy on decisions formulated in phrases such as "We shall examine ways… ", or "work for" or "improve our… ", etc. Such decisions would end with the comfortable feeling we've overcome our differences and are in agreement on what to write down in the protocol (for the next generation?). We must leave such self-deluding practices behind. **The Person-Centered organization needs only realistic action plans in which it is clear who will do what, how, how soon, and what exactly should happen in reality that can show us to what extent we have succeeded in reaching our goals.**

Another suggestion in this context is the following: Do not present just one proposition to accept or reject. Preferably, present two or more options, to help members become aware that if there is only one choice, then rejecting the one proposition means doing nothing. If there is only one proposition and the group rejects it, it should be understood that the other option is accepted, namely, the unexpressed proposition that things should stay as they are, and we will do nothing. It is important to be aware of that. For example, if the group needs to make a decision on an issue that concerns the whole Movement, I would suggest that you present it as proposition A against proposition B. Proposition B may be some version of "Things will remain as they are", and nothing will change. If proposition B is accepted, even that should not be understood as doing nothing, but be followed by posting next to it a note specifying who is going to carry it out how and how soon. For example, display the name of the person who would inform the Web's office of the group's decision.

The Strategy Tool for Direct Challenge

Using that practical tool would often make the difference between success and failure in reaching your goals. This strategic tool can be used by individuals in personal situations, but also by teams and groups whenever success depends on the help or consent of others. The tool was developed on the basis of Kurt Lewin's Force-Field Analysis (Lewin, 1948) and on some strategic principles of Gandhian Nonviolent Direct Action. Consider it a gift that you may use in personal, even intimate, situations – not just in planning political moves. I regard it as my tool and gear to carry with me in all my life struggles. Each time I forgot or neglected to use it I have regretted it.

As a democratic political power organization, your success will mostly depend on influencing people from outside your movement to join you and to support your campaigns. Your growth in power, necessary for becoming an important factor in politics as well as for your feeling of success in a political struggle, will depend on reaching out to people. "*The deliberative sense of the community should govern*" of course; your job as a political organization is to make that sense govern your way. Convincing others to support and join you is what truly democratic politics is all about. It is a formidable task, and the Strategy Tool for Direct Challenge helps in just that.

STRATEGY TOOL FOR DIRECT CHALLENGE

1. **What is your *practical* goal?** What exactly is the result you wish to attain with other persons (the other side) in the meeting (or as an

answer to a letter)? What exactly should the other side say, sign, promise, agree to, give, do, etc. to make you feel that you have gotten what you wanted? – Fill in your response in such words that as soon as the confrontation is over you will know whether or not you have reached your practical goal.
Categorically, do not begin to take action if you don't know what your practical goal is and how you will know whether or not you have reached it. Otherwise, you could easily delude yourself into believing that you did something that contributed to your cause, while in reality you did nothing of the sort. Many social-change groups mostly launch projects such that the only achievement in doing them is that they took place and made them feel accomplished. Avoid making decisions like planning demonstrations or staging a street happening only because "something has to be done".

2. **What is your *alternative* practical goal?** If, in the course of the confrontation, you realized that it was impossible to attain your goal – what would be your alternative goal? – The alternative practical goal needs to be an achievement, so that the result of choosing it would not be zero. All or nothing alternatives are more risky.

3. **What is the *heart* of your claim?** What is its strongest point, prepared in advance and worded briefly but clearly and decisively? – The "heart" of the claim is what gives you the greatest feelings of confidence and strength in putting it forth. Think about the heart of your claim as the most necessary equipment you take with you for surmounting possible obstacles on the way to achieving your goal, your strongest argument in the planned encounter or confrontation.

To think through comprehensively and know in depth the heart of your claim is crucial, because it is about your inner strength. After memorizing it well you should feel positively stronger and more confident inside. If you do not – then start to think over what the heart of your claim is. If this does not help, you would do well to either postpone the encounter or change your practical goal.

---

4. What would you say or do in the case that, in the course of dialogue, the other side did not budge from its negative attitude and you decided to terminate the encounter? **What would you say last?**

---

5. **What are the obstacles ahead?** – Take into account technical obstacles ("He's not available now", "This is not our business", etc.), real reasons that the other side might put forward to explain their disagreement with you, and difficulties that originate in the character of persons.

---

6. **What should you avoid? –** Facts, arguments, terms, estimations, strategies, etc. that you need to be careful not to use in the encounter.

---

7. **What exactly are your demands on the other side?** What would you answer if the other side responds by saying something like, "OK, what is it exactly that you want me to do?" – Be sure you know not just what but also how and how soon.

8. **Who are the potential supportive forces** (persons, organizations, institutions) that you could ask for support before the Confrontation in order to increase the chances to achieve your goals.

9. **Who are the negative forces** that you could influence directly or indirectly in preparation for the Direct Challenge in order to neutralize their negative impact on your chances to achieve your goals?

10. **What would you do next if you have not succeeded in reaching any of your goals in that Challenge?**

* * *

Please remember that the Strategy Tool for Direct Challenge is applicable in personal situations. You can use it whenever you decide to confront someone directly to get them to grant your wish or accept your proposal. It could increase your sense of well-being and make a big difference in both the experience of an encounter and the results.

FEEDBACK

The term "Feedback" originated in computer science. It does not carry any political associations. It would serve us well in conveying the idea of something new and unprecedented in political life as we know it. It is, in this author's opinion, the single most important contribution that Applied Behavioral Science can draw on to improve the quality of life for people engaged in working together and making decisions democratically as equals.

Within the framework of the Egalitarian Group Working Process, feedback has to be the last item on the agenda. However, *it is not a decision-making process*, and not all elements of the working process apply to it. Feedback-time is not decision-making, but rather a reflection of it. The group does not discuss issues that belong to its political agenda, but only issues that are vital for its own life. It needs feedback for its human survival just as a living organism needs oxygen and water. Members need it for overcoming difficulties and conflicts between them and for giving support to one another. Things said during feedback sessions should find their way to hearts and minds, not to the protocol book or other records.

Feedback is the information people get about their own behavior here and now. The decision whether to accept that information and change something in one's behavior as a result is the individual's, not the group's or anyone else's. Only when one's behavior becomes an item on the agenda can the group make a decision on it. If it is raised during feedback, nobody except the person to whom it is directed can decide anything about it.

Structurally, feedback is that period at the end of the group's working time during which the group discusses the session that has just ended, while the interpersonal events, which are the substance and the evidence of Feedback, are still fresh in memory. Participants in a Feedback session can express openly their opinions and feelings about the part they and others played in the events that took place during the group's meeting and had an effect on the process for better or worse.

"Feedback" is talking openly on what is going on among us, who and what helps and who and what hinders the group's work or hurts individuals' feelings. Its purpose is in resolving personal and interpersonal problems, easing conflicts, clarifying misunderstandings, finding constructive channels for expressing anger and frustration positively and honestly. Feelings and opinions about everything that is regularly held back, or said behind one's back, or accumulated until it poisons the atmosphere and the relationships, or erupts in aggressiveness at the least suitable time – all these can be channeled to feedback while memory is still fresh.

Feedback in groups has a very strong effect. By the mechanism of feedback, grownups can receive information about reality they would never know otherwise. That is among the most important forms of information one can get in life: information about how others really perceive, understand, and evaluate us. Feedback is a conscious effort to do something about the cultural situation, in which we all tend to more easily see the defects of others and be blind in admitting them in ourselves.

Authoritarian people, bosses, leaders, do not want their defects to be pointed out, because they want their subordinates' praise and "respect" (in politics, it is mostly based on calculations of self-interest and on fear). They consequently try to avoid and block any criticism. Hence, the language of political criticism is aggressive and primitive, and is hardly ever helpful. But as far as the Person-Centered organization is concerned – NO MORE OF THAT! One thing seems certain: if feedback sessions were held at the end of meetings of any powerful political organization, on any level from a local Party branch to the national government, political experience as we know it would be radically changed.

Feedback is rare in most areas of culture. It takes a high level of intellectual and emotional effort and requires considerable skills in interrelations. Empathetic listening, openness, and assertiveness in self-expression are some of them. For group members it will function as an effective antidote against individual tendencies to dominate, manipulate, depreciate or control others. Psychologically conflicted people who need very thick defensive walls to protect them against the truth about themselves would be particularly offended and may choose to leave. However, it would always remain the real touchstone of quality in the group's life. People who are normally open, willing to learn and less afraid to make changes will find group-feedback to be their most valuable tool for personal growth.

True feedback frequently hurts the recipient because personal change in a relationship does not come easy. Yet, done properly it could be given and received as an act of true loving care and could generate positive feelings in people. A democratic-egalitarian group that succeeded in integrating feedback into its life processes could consider itself as having an incomparably higher quality of life than any conventional group, political or otherwise. It would then have a chance to attract capable people, overcome its difficulties, and succeed in reaching its goals without degenerating to mere power and conflict relationships.

THE PRACTICE OF FEEDBACK

Group feedback is structured behavior based on theory, research, experience and know-how that requires learning and practice. The learning is "experiential", meaning people learn from their own experience with others in the group. Frameworks of such experiential learning are "T-groups" ("T" for training) that focus on Group Dynamics. Many professional and paraprofessional people can serve as facilitators for Affinity Groups, and their intervention would be very much welcomed in the initial stages of the group's life. The major reason for that is that feedback runs against the most deeply rooted social habits in human relations.

Normal interpersonal relations rest on conventions built around the principle of authority by which one should not voice personal remarks directly in the face of other persons, and if one does, it must take the form of a personal attack. Feeding back personal remarks directly is associated with the use of aggressiveness, while feedback should be the opposite of this. It should serve as an instrument for helping to solve interpersonal problems and heal interpersonal injuries. A climate of security and trust must prevail, because people under attack cannot learn. An external professional facilitator who is impartial regarding conflicts in the group can facilitate such a supportive climate. Feedback is the medium for the development of skills in interpersonal relations that lead to "personal growth" and, by extension, to "Organizational Development" toward a higher quality of organizational life.

The profound change of attitudes and habits, associated with turning away from the usual patterns of interpersonal dealings toward feedback, is the reason why professional help should be welcomed. For the benefit of Affinity Groups that don't have members experienced in giving and receiving feedback, here are some of the accepted techniques for conducting feedback sessions. I shall briefly explain the commonly given reasons for using these techniques:

- Better to ask for feedback than give it to a person who has not asked for it. At the beginning, in particular, it is good to start with a person *asking* for feedback. For example, a natural and good way is that the chairperson asks for feedback that would evaluate his or her recent performance on the job, what could be done differently, better, etc.
- It is better to offer feedback to a person and get an agreement to provide it than to impose it on an unwilling person. I would recommend the following rule-of-thumb: whenever person A wants to criticize person B, he/she should first ask B if she/he wants or can accept feedback here-and-now. If B is not up to it, B may be given the option not to receive it at that session. If feedback is "dumped" on someone who is not ready and willing to receive it, the chances of it being helpful would be considerably less.
- Give "positive" supportive feedback, such as serves to commend and strengthen another person's behavior, if she or he truly deserves it. Criticism and praise stem from contrasting emotions and elicit contrasting emotional responses. For the sake of balancing the atmosphere of feed-

back, if not for its own sake, it is advisable to remember the full half of the proverbial half-empty glass. Most people want to be liked, reinforced and appreciated; this is an important element of what amounts to a good social climate and organizational quality of life. It also helps to open peoples' hearts to constructive criticism, though even the most useful criticism, or "negative feedback", might hurt.

- In groups where open personal feedback might seem too threatening, impersonal group feedback could be used. It could begin by each person responding anonymously to a short feedback questionnaire. The written feedback could include items such as questions about what was the low point of that group meeting, what was the high point, who contributed most, what impeded progress, etc. Then it is summed-up, and the results presented as the basis for a general discussion.

"**If I've understood you correctly ...** " – The master-key technique for re-connecting broken lines of interpersonal communication.

That technique of "Empathetic Listening" is employed like this: Before B responds to A, B must first repeat the essentials of what A has said and has to get A's agreement that A feels understood. B is not allowed to speak his/her own mind before she or he has that confirmation from A.

In direct personal feedback this rule is highly recommended. That means, that if B agrees to receive personal feedback from A, B must first, before responding, summarize A's feedback and get A's confirmation that he or she has been understood correctly. Only after the receiver of feedback has gotten that confirmation from the giver can the receiver respond. It helps the giver of feedback not to be misunderstood and the receiver not to rush into self-defense, but take time to reflect on the feedback and become less emotionally threatened.

I have hardly ever experienced that using the "master-key" technique has had bad effects or was not beneficial for all parties. The technique is like a brake we can always engage when there is a danger of collision or accident. The "**If I've understood you correctly ...** " mode broadcasts openness and real willingness to listen. It would be decoded as if the person said, "Your opinion about my behavior is important to me, and I wish to make sure I understand it well before I respond". Then, when we as speakers get confirmation that we were really understood, it gives us a feeling of being humanly valued, which is crucial for productive criticism. Not *really* listening is how people devalue one another most frequently; being criticized while feeling you were altogether not listened to and have been misunderstood is a common experience of feeling devalued.

The American psychologist Marshall Rosenberg dedicated his life to spreading the message of Nonviolent Communication. He did it particularly in the most troubled parts of the world, torn by war and violence, and he did it in such a charming way that I feel privileged to have participated in one of his workshops in Israel and to link you with him. Here is the link to one of his videotaped introductory presentations on YouTube: https://youtu.be/l7TONauJGfc. At the very beginning, you will hear him sing a song with lyrics that to me best explain the merits of Nonviolent Communication, including the "Master Key" technique in giving and receiving feedback:

I never feel more given to than when you take from me
And you understand the joy I feel caring for you
And you know my giving isn't done to put you in my debt
But because I want to live the love I feel for you.

To receive with grace may be the greatest giving
There's no way that I can separate the two
When you give to me I give you my receiving
And when you take from me I feel so given to.

(While watching, observe his body posture, facial expressions, the fact that in his role as a lecturer and teacher Marshall chose to sing to his audience, as clues to what he was "telling" about the heavy issues discussed in this book, like leadership, natural leadership, institutionalized leadership and charisma.)

The "master-key" is only a technique, but it compels the user to *listen*. You cannot fake it, if you were not listening you would not be able to summarize what the other person said, and you would not get his or her consent that you understood her or him correctly. Listening is the oxygen in the atmosphere of human communication. Using the same image, political interpersonal communication as we know it works on pure carbon dioxide; listening is considered weakness, trying to force your views on the other person (the "opponent") is the rule. Let us leave this manipulative game behind us once and for all.

THE RIGHT TO EFFECT A SHORT PERIOD OF SILENCE – A COMMUNICATION SAFETY VALVE

Give the Right to effect a short silence of 30 seconds or more to every group member once or twice in a meeting, at any time the individual wants, with no other member having a right to object. Granting individuals this right requires courage to break, for the first time, a lifelong cultural habit. After that it becomes easy. Its purpose is to give yet more respect and power to every individual and every individual is bound to feel it. In terms of the group process, the purpose is to tap every source of human energy in each of us for directing it, in tense moments, back to the sources of self-control, reflection, rationality, listening, and awareness of self and others here-and-now. This technique would help prevent the outbreak of noise characteristic of defensiveness, aggressiveness, and anxiety. The flow of discussion will be discontinued for a short time (30 silent seconds feel very long, though, in such circumstances . . .) that is insignificant in comparison to all the time dedicated to decision-making, but could be very significant in avoiding dangerous collisions or preventing derailing discussions.

* * *

A REFLECTION ON THE CHANCES THAT A PERSON-CENTERED POLITICAL ORGANIZATION BECOMES REALITY

> *In presenting the idea I must face a danger. If I refrain from divulging any of my thoughts about its chances to materialize in the future, it could be understood that I myself have no faith in it. And if I take the opposite course, and firmly claim my faith in its materialization, I might be taken for a spinner of an imaginary web. – Theodore Hertzel.*

That has been the Blueprint for political power organizations free of power corruption. As the Organizational Development consultant of the Person-centered political organization, I have at this point finished my intervention. Now you have the entire recipe in front of your eyes. You can begin your journey in the terrain, knowing that you are equipped with the best road-map available in Applied Behavioral Science and some related fields, for making decisions and implementing them while preventing inequality in the distribution of power. You have the means of avoiding the pitfalls and slippery terrain that can drive you off the Person-Centered road into the Party-politicking hell of power corruption. I fully believe that the suggested group process can work well for people with a Person-Centered spirit; I have experienced group-work myself in what I regard as the best times of my life, full of personal growth and achievement, creativity, and human affinity.

In suggesting the application of some ideas and tools that were developed in the scientific field of human behavior but so far not applied in political organizations, I have already confronted the characteristic expressions of resistance to change, a well-documented phenomenon in the professional field: "Say, do you think that it can work here, in *our* situation?" "Can it work in the Middle East?" "Is it compatible with human nature, modern life, our culture?" "Has it really worked in America?", etc., etc… – endless variations on the theme of resistance to change into something new which has not yet been established.

Though I cannot predict the fate of the idea of political web-organization in the future any more than anyone else, I shall briefly address this subject matter, as I do not wish to be thought of as trying to avoid the issue which for me is so crucial.

It always makes one feel good to be able to associate one's situation with that of great personages who *did* make it. Therefore, I like to recall what a man once said whose vision at the time seemed utterly fantastic: Theodore Hertzel, the man quoted at the opening of this section. The quotation appeared in his introduction to a little brochure that no respectable publisher in Vienna was willing to publish at the end of the 19th century: "*The Jewish State*". Hertzel put it simply, "*The actualization of the idea is dependent only on the number of people who would follow it*". Paraphrasing his most famous saying, "*If you will – that is not a fairy tale*" – I could say to you, "If you *won't* – that *is* a fairy-tale… " – a 'fairy tale' which, however, will not pass from the face of the earth but in this or some other form be transfigured and await its time.

Secondly, it can be safely predicted that once a living example of political web-organization exists, its chances of expanding and attracting many more people will be much better than our present chance to see it come to life. It is a well known finding that it is much easier to persuade people to follow a path which somebody has created and got somewhere than starting to pave their own new path in a terrain, particularly such a treacherous terrain as politics. In fact, I suppose (no objectivity in this supposition) that when the Web Organization of small groups becomes an option it would take a very peculiar kind of idealistic youth to join a political party or a movement as we know them today.

We may take the Israeli Kibbutz movement as a case in point. Some hundreds of thousands of people, five generations, living in economic and social equality incomparably greater than their surroundings, comparatively happy, free; practically free of the severe problems which plague societies such as unscrupulous competition, abysmal economic inequality, poverty, racism and violent crime. If they had not existed – would anyone believe that such an idea of communal living could exist? And if they *were* organized as a person-centered web of independent communes – would they ever fall into the crisis they experienced and which disintegrated their communality and equality? – Based on my deep personal involvement and inside knowledge in the first half of my life, they would not! They would rather expand and attract many more people in many countries in the world who would see in their existence a living example of community based on the values of personal freedom, socio-economic equality and interpersonal solidarity, fraternity and affinity.

In reality, the founders and members of the Zionist communal movement were tragically oblivious to the iniquities, injustice, and *psychological* exploitation inherent in *an unequal* distribution of influence and power, even while their distribution of material goods was equal. Feeling that they could not really share in decision-making that would shape their destiny, many opted out. In the blessed absence of physical coercion (such as afflicted their siblings and cousins who stayed in the Soviet Union), alienation and powerlessness settled in, breeding indifference and passivity. The kibbutz society lost its faith in self-direction and begun drifting along with everything around it.

My kibbutz-family members never had any realistic conceptions about the dangers of being true believers, about interpersonal and organizational dynamics, about political power, *psychological* exploitation and political influence… Mentally they remained disciples of ideological idols like their parents, Jewish religious Hasidim or their cousins the Communists. Those young pioneers of a better world are all dead now. For me, this

Blueprint is an attempt to correct what they did not understand and did not practice.

I feel intellectually indebted and close in heart to the pioneer of humanistic political psychology Erich Fromm, who advanced the idea of the web political organization made up of small face-to-face groups. He died without seeing it materialize, but passed the torch on. He had written the words that, one by one, express my feelings about the future, even while I work to publish his ideas again:

> *I believe no man can save his fellow man by making the choice for him. All that one can do for his fellow man is presenting the alternatives faithfully and lovingly but without sentimentality or illusion. The confrontation of people with the real possibilities in their lives might awaken the potential powers of a person and enable him to choose life rather than self-destruction. If he is not able to choose life no one can breathe life into him.* – Erich Fromm – *Beyond the Chains of Illusion.*

* * *

REFERENCES

Atlee, Tom (2000), *The Tao of Democracy*, Eugene, OR: The Co-Intelligence Institute.

Argyris, Chris (1971), *Management an Organizational Development*, New York: McGraw Hall.

Buber, Martin (1948), *Between Man and Man*, New York: Macmillan, p. 202.

Bradford, Leland D., Gibb, Jack R. and Benne, Kenneth D. (1964), *T-Group Theory and Laboratory Method*, New York: John Wiley & Sons.

Bennis, Warren G., Benne, Kennet D. and Chin, Robert (1984), *The Planning of Change 4th Edition*, New York: Holt, Rinehart & Winston.

Bennis, W. G., Schein E. et al. (1964), *Interpersonal Dynamics, Homewood, IL: The Dorsey Press.*

Fromm, Erich (1955), *The Sane Society*, New York: Holt, Rinehart & Winston.

Fromm, Erich (1962), *Beyond the Chains of Illusion*, New York: Simon and Schuster, p. 176.

Galbraith, J. K. (1973), *Economics and the Public Purpose*, Boston: Houghton Mifflin Co.

Huxley, Aldous (1958), *Brave New World Revisited*, New York: Harper & Brothers.

Lewin, Kurt. *Resolving Social Conflicts*, New York: Harper & Brothers, 1948.

Luft, J. (1970), *Group Processes: An Introduction to Group Dynamics*, Palo Alto, CA: Mayfield Publishing Company.

Merry, U. and Allerhand M. E. (1977), *Developing Teams and Organizations*, Reading, MA: Addison Wesley.

Mumford, Lewis (1973), *The Condition of Man*, New York: Harcourt Brace Jovanovich.

Postman, Neil (1986). *Amusing Ourselves to Death*, New York: Penguin, (1986).

Rogers, Carl. (1970). *On Encounter Groups,* New York: Harrow Books, *Harper and Row.*

Rogers, Carl. (1977). Carl Rogers o*n Personal Power: Inner Strength and Its Revolutionary Impact*, New York: Dell Publishing Co.

Schein, Edgar H., *Process Consultation* (1969), Reading, MA: Addison Wesley